Girls Play

Girls
JOIN THE
TEAM

LACROSSE

Kate Rogers

PowerKiDS press

New York

Published in 2017 by The Rosen Publishing Group, Inc.
29 East 21st Street, New York, NY 10010

First Edition

Editor: Katie Kawa
Book Design: Tanya Dellaccio

Photo Credits: Cover, p. 17 Mitchell Layton/Getty Images; p. 5 (top) Larry St. Pierre/Shuterstock.com; p. 5 (bottom) https://commons.wikimedia.org/wiki/File:George_Catlin_-_Ball-play_of_the_Choctaw–Ball_Up_-_Google_Art_Project.jpg; p. 7 Past Pix/Getty Images; p. 9 (top) https://commons.wikimedia.org/wiki/File:Lacrosse_at_the_Olympics,_London,_1948._(7649951098).jpg; p. 9 (bottom) Joe Amon/Getty Images; pp. 13, 22 Brian McEntire/Shutterstock.com; p. 15 (top) Aspen Photo/Shutterstock.com; p. 15 (bottom) Alan C. Heison/Shutterstock.com; p. 19 (top) Rich Barnes/Getty Images; p. 19 (bottom) Bill Frakes/Getty Images; p. 21 Karl Gehring/Getty Images.

Cataloging-in-Publication Data

Names: Rogers, Kate.
Title: Girls play lacrosse / Kate Rogers.
Description: New York : PowerKids Press, 2017. | Series: Girls join the team | Includes index.
Identifiers: ISBN 9781499421019 (pbk.) | ISBN 9781499421033 (library bound) | ISBN 9781499421026 (6 pack)
Subjects: LCSH: Lacrosse for women–Juvenile literature. | Lacrosse for children–Juvenile literature.
Classification: LCC GV989.15 R64 2017 | DDC 796.34'7082–d23

Manufactured in the United States of America

CPSIA Compliance Information: Batch #BS16PK For Further Information contact Rosen Publishing, New York, New York at 1-800-237-9932

CONTENTS

A SPEEDY SPORT

Lacrosse is a fast-paced sport that's fun to play and exciting to watch. It's also one of the fastest-growing sports for young people to play in the United States.

Lacrosse started as a Native American sport. It's now a sport played by men and women around the world. In fact, more girls are playing lacrosse today than ever before. Girls who play lacrosse learn more than just passing and shooting skills. They learn to work together toward a goal. Does that sound like fun? Read on to learn more about the speedy sport of lacrosse!

Overtime!

When Native Americans would gather to play lacrosse many years ago, a game could last for days and feature thousands of players.

Lacrosse has changed from its earliest days, but it's still a sport that calls for fast feet and quick thinking.

GROWING THE GAME

The modern sport of lacrosse has its roots in games played with sticks and a ball by native peoples who lived in Canada and the northeastern United States. Europeans were introduced to early versions, or kinds, of lacrosse when they came to North America. By the mid-1800s, men's lacrosse clubs had formed in Canada. The sport also began to grow in other countries, including the United States.

Women's lacrosse is believed to have started at St. Leonard's School in Scotland in 1890. Rosabelle Sinclair, who studied at this school, played a big part in the growth of women's lacrosse in the United States.

Overtime!

In 1926, Rosabelle Sinclair began teaching young women to play lacrosse at the Bryn Mawr School in Baltimore, Maryland. That school has the longest-running girls' lacrosse program in the United States.

As women's lacrosse became more popular, groups were created to govern the sport. The first of these governing bodies in the United States—the United States Women's Lacrosse Association—was founded in 1931.

INTERNATIONAL PLAY

Men's lacrosse had become popular enough by the start of the 1900s to be officially included in the 1904 and 1908 Summer Olympics. It was also played as a **demonstration sport** in the 1928, 1932, and 1948 Olympics. However, Olympic officials didn't believe there was enough international interest in men's lacrosse to make it a **permanent** part of the Olympic Games again. Women's lacrosse has never been an Olympic sport.

Instead, the best women's lacrosse players in the world face each other every four years in the Women's Lacrosse World Cup. The U.S. women's lacrosse team is the most successful team in World Cup history.

Overtime!

As of 2016, the United States has come in either first or second in every Women's Lacrosse World Cup since an international **championship** was first held in 1982.

men's lacrosse in the 1948 Olympics

Many believe that both men's and women's lacrosse are now popular enough all over the world to become part of the Summer Olympics. Until then, the world's greatest players **represent** their countries in other international contests, including the World Cup.

THE RULES OF THE GAME

The object of the game of lacrosse is simple enough: to get the ball into the other team's goal. Each goal is worth one point. The only lacrosse player who can touch the ball with her hands is the goalkeeper. This means players have to use their stick to throw the ball into the goal.

Women's lacrosse games feature 12 players on each team. These players are divided into four groups: attack players, midfielders, defensive players, and the goalkeeper. They all have to work together in order to score and keep the other team from scoring.

Overtime!

Cradling is a special skill used in lacrosse that involves turning the stick using the arms and wrists. This allows a player to have control over the ball when it's in her stick.

attack players

make offensive (goal-scoring) plays

★ first home: scores goals

★ second home: creates scoring chances for herself and her teammates

★ third home: passes the ball to move the play from defense to offense and can also score goals

defensive players

keep other team from scoring

★ point: marks (guards) the other team's first home

★ cover point: marks the other team's second home

★ third man: marks the other team's third home and breaks up passes

LACROSSE POSITIONS

midfielders

play both offense and defense

★ attack wings: move the ball quickly from defense to offense

★ defense wings: mark the other team's attack wings

★ center: plays both offense and defense and controls the draw (the fight for the ball after play is stopped)

goalkeeper

keeps the ball from going in the goal, can use her hands

A women's lacrosse team has two attack wings and two defense wings, as well as one of each of the other positions. Which position would you like to play?

LACROSSE GEAR

The most important piece of equipment, or gear, needed to play lacrosse is a stick. In fact, lacrosse got its name because it's a sport played with sticks. "La crosse" was the word the French used to describe a bishop's staff, which is what French-speaking settlers thought lacrosse sticks looked like. A lacrosse stick is still sometimes called a crosse. The head of the stick has a net that can hold the ball.

The ball is also an important part of a lacrosse game. In women's lacrosse, the ball is most often yellow.

Overtime!

Goalkeepers wear extra equipment because they often get hit by the hard ball traveling at high speeds. This addtional equipment includes a helmet, gloves, and chest **protector**.

Women's lacrosse players must wear a mouth guard to protect their teeth as well as something to protect their eyes. If they want to, they can also wear gloves and soft headgear.

WHAT'S DIFFERENT?

Some of the biggest differences between men's and women's lacrosse involve the equipment used to play the game. Men's lacrosse sticks have a part called a pocket, which is deep enough to hold the ball securely. Women's lacrosse sticks can't have a pocket. This makes it easier to lose the ball.

Men's lacrosse players are allowed to push the player who has the ball and hit players with their stick at certain times. This isn't allowed in women's lacrosse. Because of this, all men's lacrosse players have to wear helmets, while only goalkeepers in women's lacrosse wear them.

Overtime!

Indoor lacrosse, or box lacrosse, is a version of this sport most often played only by men. There are some women's indoor lacrosse teams, but outdoor, or field, lacrosse is the most popular version among women.

men's lacrosse

There are some important differences between men's and women's lacrosse, but both need players who are speedy and smart.

COLLEGE LACROSSE

If you enjoy playing lacrosse and work hard to be the best player you can be, you might be able to play this sport in college. Women's participation in college sports, including lacrosse, began to grow after a law called Title IX, or Title Nine, was passed in 1972. This law states schools that receive money from the **federal** government have to give girls and women the same opportunities as boys and men to play sports.

In 1982, the **National Collegiate Athletic Association** (NCAA) began holding a championship for women's lacrosse. The University of Maryland has won more NCAA women's lacrosse championships than any other school.

Overtime!

As of 2015, there were 103 teams playing at the highest level of women's college lacrosse in the United States.

From 1995 to 2001, the University of Maryland's women's lacrosse team won seven NCAA championships in a row!

A RECORD-SETTING PLAYER

Jen Adams was one of the stars of the University of Maryland's lacrosse team during its run of seven straight championships. She's known as the best women's lacrosse player of all time. Jen, who was born in Australia, played for Maryland from 1998 to 2001. She was the national player of the year three times while she was in college.

After college, Jen won a gold **medal** and two silver medals playing for Australia in the World Cup. She also started coaching. She helped coach at colleges, including the University of Maryland, before becoming the head women's lacrosse coach at Loyola University Maryland.

Overtime!

As of 2015, Jen Adams holds the NCAA record for most points scored in her college **career** with 445 points.

Jen Adams coaching for Loyola

Jen Adams believes in growing the sport of lacrosse by introducing it to kids around the world. She's said, "We've got to get sticks in the hands of more kids across the globe!"

A NEW LEAGUE

Until 2016, there were no **professional** opportunities for women who wanted to keep playing lacrosse after college. Then, the United Women's Lacrosse **League** (UWLX) was formed and began playing games. This league started with teams from Baltimore, Maryland; Boston, Massachusetts; Long Island, New York; and Philadelphia, Pennsylvania.

The UWLX was created by a group of people who believe there should be more professional women's sports teams and leagues. Lacrosse was a good choice for a professional league because of its rising popularity among young people—especially girls—in the United States.

Overtime!

More than 100 jobs in the UWLX—from athletes to coaches to the league's commissioner, or leader— were created to give women a stronger presence in the world of professional sports.

The UWLX gives girls who love lacrosse a new goal to work toward.

EVERYBODY WINS!

Lacrosse is a sport that's growing all over the world. In the United States, it's becoming increasingly popular with young athletes. It's continuing to grow at the college level, too. Also, thanks to the UWLX, girls can now dream of playing lacrosse professionally after they finish school.

Playing lacrosse helps girls in more ways than just keeping them active. If you play lacrosse, you learn the importance of teamwork and never giving up—even when the game gets hard. When girls learn those valuable lessons, everybody wins!

GLOSSARY

career: A period of time spent doing a job or activity.

championship: A contest to find out who's the best player or team in a sport.

demonstration sport: A sport played during the Olympics that doesn't count toward the official medal total and is most often a popular sport from the host country.

federal: Relating to the central government of the United States.

league: A group of teams that play the same sport and compete against each other.

medal: A flat, small piece of metal with art or words that's used as an honor or reward.

National Collegiate Athletic Association: The organization that governs college sports in the United States.

permanent: Lasting for a long time; not changing.

professional: Having to do with a job someone does for a living.

protector: Something that keeps someone or something safe.

represent: To act officially for someone or something.

INDEX

WEBSITES

Due to the changing nature of Internet links, PowerKids Press has developed
an online list of websites related to the subject of this book. This site is
updated regularly. Please use this link to access the list:
www.powerkidslinks.com/gjt/lax